175 Sermon Outlines

175 Sermon Outlines

John Lewis Mayshack

Baker Book House
Grand Rapids, Michigan

ISBN: 0-8010-6085-0

Seventeenth printing, Oct 2005

Printed in the United States of America

For information about academic books, resources for Christain leaders, and
all new releases available from Baker Book House, visit our web site:
http://www.bakerbooks.com

1
IN THIS I GLORY

"But God forbid that I should glory, save in the cross of our Lord Jesus Christ, by whom the world is crucified unto me, and I unto the world." Galatians 6:14

1. Some Glory in Riches
2. Some Glory in Wisdom
3. Some Glory in Power
4. Paul's Glory—The Cross of Christ

2
THE WINDOWS OF MOTHERHOOD

"Moreover, his mother made him a little coat, and brought it to him from year to year, when she came up with her husband to offer the yearly sacrifice." I Samuel 2:19

1. The Window of Faith
2. The Window of Virtue
3. The Window of Love
4. The Window of Prayer

3
WATCHMAN, WHAT OF THE NIGHT?

"The burden of Dumah. He calleth to me out of Seir, Watchman, what of the night? Watchman, what of the night?" Isaiah 21:11

1. The Long Night of Anxiety
2. The Dark Night of Personal Tragedy
3. The Glorious Night of Salvation

4
A GOOD GOD FOR BAD TIMES

The times in which we now live challenge the very core of our existence. There is not a single structure of contemporary civilization that has escaped the crucial tests of today's changing world. The central theme of Psalm 46 is that God remains as our source of strength even in bad times.

1. Something to Know (God *Is*) v. 1
2. Something to Believe (The Lord of Hosts Is with Us) v. 7
3. Something to See (Come Behold the Works of the Lord) v. 8
4. Something to Witness (The Exaltation of God) v. 10

5

IS LIFE WORTH LIVING?

"But I am a worm, and no man; a reproach of men, and despised of the people." Psalm 22:6

1. Life Is Worth Living when We Maintain a Positive Self-image
2. Life Is Worth Living when We Reach Out to Other People
3. Life is Worth Living when We Seek God's Guidance

6

WHAT THE LORD REQUIRES

"He hath shewed thee, O man, what is good; and what doth the Lord require of thee, but to do justly, and to love mercy, and to walk humbly with thy God?" Micah 6:8

1. God Requires Us to Be Just in Our Dealings
2. God Requires Us to Be Lovers of Mercy
3. God Requires Us to Walk Humbly Before Him

7

OF THIS I AM CERTAIN

"For we brought nothing into this world, and it is certain we can carry nothing out." I Timothy 6:7

1. We Brought Nothing into this World
2. This World Is Not Our Home
3. Life Ushers Us Out with Nothing

8

A BLIND BEGGAR'S FAITH

"And he cried, saying, Jesus, thou son of David, have mercy on me." Luke 18:38

1. The Beggar's Request (Have mercy on me) v. 38
2. The Beggar's Persistence (He cried so much the more) v. 39
3. The Beggar's Response to Christ (He followed Christ) v. 43

9

PEARLS OF WISDOM

"Wherefore, my beloved brethren, let every man be swift to hear, slow to speak, slow to wrath." James 1:19

Every Christian should be:
1. Swift to Hear
2. Slow to Speak
3. Slow to Wrath

10

FORGIVENESS

"Then came Peter to him, and said, Lord, how oft shall my brother sin against me, and I forgive him? till seven times? Matthew 18:21

1. Forgiveness Has No Limitations
2. He Who Does Not Forgive Is Not Forgiven
3. The Need for Forgiveness Is Universal

5

11

THE LOVE OF GOD

"For God so loved the world, that he gave his only begotten Son, that whosoever believeth in him should not perish, but have everlasting life." John 3:16

1. God Loves Us with a Love that Keeps on Loving
2. God Loves Us with a Love that Keeps on Giving
3. God Loves Us with a Love that Keps Reaching Out to Save Us

12

WHICH SIDE ARE YOU ON?

"Then was Jesus led up of the spirit into the wilderness to be tempted of the devil." Matthew 4:1

1. Your Commitment Needs to Be Clear
2. God Has an Investment in You
3. The Crucial Hour Is at Hand

13

THE VOICE THAT QUIETS YOUR FEARS

"And after the earthquake a fire; but the Lord was not in the fire: and after the fire a still small voice." I Kings 19:12

God will come to us,
1. When We Feel Alone Against the World
2. When it Seems as if We Have Given All
3. When the Road Ahead Seems Unclear

14

RENEWAL IN THE WILDERNESS

"As it is written in the book of the words of Esaias the prophet, saying, The voice of one crying in the wilderness, Prepare ye the way of the Lord, make his paths straight." Luke 3:4

Renewal takes place when there is:
1. An Acute Sense of the Presence of God
2. A Working Knowledge of Things as They Ought to Be
3. An Awareness of One's Role in the Divine Plan

15

CHRIST, OUR REDEEMING LORD

"And he was numbered with the transgressors; and he bare the sin of many, and made intercession for the transgressors." Isaiah 53:12

1. Christ Poured Out His Soul until Death
2. Christ Was Numbered with the Transgressors
3. Christ Now Intercedes for Transgressors

16

DON'T LOSE CHRIST

"And when they had fulfilled the days, as they returned, the child Jesus tarried behind in Jerusalem; and Joseph and his mother knew not of it." Luke 2:43

1. Don't Lose Christ Because of Anger
2. Don't Lose Christ by Taking a Short-cut
3. Don't Lose Christ by Fearing to Accept His Challenge

17

IT TOOK A MIRACLE

"And he fell to the earth, and heard a voice saying unto him, Saul, Saul, why persecutest thou me?" Acts 9:4

1. It Took a Miracle to Claim Paul's Attention
2. It Took a Miracle to Save Paul's Soul
3. It Took a Miracle to Claim Paul's Loyalty

18

WHY ARE YOU HERE?

"And he came thither unto a cave, and lodged there; and, behold, the word of the Lord came to him, and he said unto him, What doest thou here, Elijah?" I Kings 19:9

We should not retreat when we discover that:
1. God Has Been Our Keeper
2. There Are Others Who Share Our Faith
3. Life's Last Chapter Is Yet Unwritten

19

REDIGGING OLD WELLS

"And Isaac digged again the wells of water, which they had digged in the days of Abraham his father." Genesis 26:18

1. The Well of Personal Integrity
2. The Well of Human Kindness
3. The Well of Hope

20

AT EASE IN ZION

"Woe to them that are at ease in Zion, and trust in the mountains of Samaria. . ." Amos 6:1

1. A Warning Against Religious Idleness
2. A Warning Against Taking God for Granted
3. A Warning Against False Security

21

GOD WILL DELIVER US

"So Daniel was taken up out of the den, and no manner of hurt was found upon him, because he believed in God." Daniel 6:23

God will deliver us:
1. When Evil Entangles Us
2. When All Seems Hopeless
3. When We Must Stand Alone

22

THE BARREN FIG TREE

"And when he saw a fig tree in the way, he came to it, and found nothing thereon, but leaves only, and said unto it, Let no fruit grow on thee henceforward for ever." Matthew 21:19

1. A Lesson About the Futility of Externalism
2. A Lesson About the Meaning of Christian Service
3. A Lesson About Our Personal Fate

23

THE MEANING OF DISCIPLESHIP

"And the disciples were called Christians first in Antioch." Acts 11:26

The disciples were called Christians because they were:
1. Men Inspired by a Personal Experience with God
2. Men Who Possessed a Strong Religious Conviction
3. Men Who Behaved with Christlike Manners

24

AN INDICTMENT AGAINST SOLEMN ASSEMBLIES

Amos 5:18–27

The indictments:
1. Big on Festivals and Little on Faith
2. Offered Sacrifices but Not Their Hearts
3. Preached Justice but Practiced Injustice

25

CONTENDERS FOR THE FAITH

"Beloved, when I gave all diligence to write unto you of the common salvation, it was needful for me to write unto you, and exhort you that ye should earnestly contend for the faith which was once delivered unto the saints." Jude 1:3

1. The Nature of Our Labor (Love)
2. The Motive of Our Labor (Salvation)
3. The Strength for Our Labor (Jesus)

26

FRIENDSHIP WITH JESUS

"And I say unto you my friends, Be not afraid of them that kill the body, and after that have no more that they can do." Luke 12:4

1. Friendship with Jesus Banishes Our Fears
2. Friendship with Jesus Makes Our Faith Fresh Every Morning
3. Friendship with Jesus Assures Us of a Glorious Future

27

GOD IS STILL IN CONTROL

Acts 12:1–11

Because we recognize that God is still in control:
1. We Are Not Afraid of Danger
2. We Are Not Afraid to Suffer
3. We Are Not Afraid to Trust God's Care

28

DON'T GIVE UP NOW

"And when he saw their faith, he said unto him, Man, thy sins are forgiven thee." Luke 5:20

1. Present Circumstances Can Be Overcome
2. There Are Friends Who Are Willing to Help you
3. God Is Waiting for You to Come to Him

29

WHAT SHALL WE DO WITH JESUS?

"Pilate saith unto them, What shall I do then with Jesus which is called Christ? They all say unto him, Let him be crucified." Matthew 27:22

1. Accept Christ as Savior
2. Trust Christ as Lord
3. Obey Christ as Master

30

THE WAGES OF SIN

"For the wages of sin is death; but the gift of God is eternal life through Jesus Christ our Lord." Romans 6:23

1. Sin Alienates Man from Himself
2. Sin Alienates Man from His Fellowman
3. Sin Alienates Man from God

31

SERVICE: A PRELUDE TO GREATNESS

"But it shall not be so among you: but whosoever will be great among you, let him be your minister." Matthew 20:26

1. The Nature of True Greatness (Service)
2. The Model of True Greatness (Jesus)
3. The Motive for True Greatness (Eternal Life)

32

A MAN FOR OUR TIMES

"Study to shew thyself approved unto God, a workman that needth not to be ashamed, rightly dividing the word of truth."
II Timothy 2:15

1. The Man Who Is Not Afraid to Study
2. The Man Who Is Not Afraid to Love
3. The Man Who Is Not Afraid to Suffer
4. The Man Who Is Not Afraid to Trust

33

WHEN LIFE'S BURDENS GET HEAVY

Psalm 142

1. Some Turn to Self-pity
2. Some Turn to a False Security
3. Some Turn to the Almighty God

34

THE SAGA OF THE BLOWING WIND

"Then said he unto me, Prophesy unto the wind, prophesy, son of man, and say to the wind, Thus saith the Lord God; Come from the four winds, O breath, and breathe upon these slain, that they may live." Ezekiel 37:9

The saga of the blowing wind tells of:
1. The Helpless Condition of Man
2. The Presence of God in Human Life
3. The Power of God over Life

35

THE WILDERNESS EXPERIENCE

Exodus 16:1–16

1. The Wilderness Experience Is a Dangerous Experience

2. The Wilderness Experience Is a Necessary Experience
3. The Wilderness Experience Shapes Us for the Promised Land

36

GOD'S REMNANT

Romans 11:1–5

1. A Remnant Is an Expression of the Grace of God
2. A Remnant Is a Visible Sign of God's Church
3. A Remnant Is the Evidence of God's Love

37

PILGRIMS OF A HIGHER HOPE

"I have given them thy word; and the world hath hated them, because they are not of the world, even as I am not of the world." John 17:14

1. Pilgrims Are People Who Have Been Uprooted
2. Pilgrims Are Foreigners in an Alien Land
3. Pilgrims Are Those Who Seek a Place of Eternal Rest

38

KEEP THE FAITH

"How shall we sing the Lord's song in a strange land?" Psalm 137:4

1. To Perpetuate a Rich Heritage
2. To Offset the Forces of Evil
3. To Be Able to Stand in the Day of Judgment

39

LIFE'S FINAL CROSSROADS

"And they came to a place which was named Gethsemane: and he saith to his disciples, Sit ye here, while I shall pray." Mark 14:32

1. Gethsemane—The Crossroad of Prayer
2. Gethsemane—The Crossroad of Betrayal
3. Gethsemane—The Crossroad of God's Will

40

THE EASTER FAITH

"He is not here, but is risen: remember how he spake unto you when he was yet in Galilee." Luke 24:6

1. The Rebirth of Hope
2. The Assurance That Good Triumphs over Evil
3. The Experience of Personal Salvation
4. Something to Share with Others

41

BY THE GRACE OF GOD

"By the grace of God I am what I am: and his grace which was bestowed upon me was not in vain: but I laboured more abundantly than they all..." I Corinthians 15:10

When we speak of the grace of God in our lives, we mean:
1. Our Inability to Reach the Mark
2. God's Compassion Toward Us
3. Our Total Dependence upon God
4. Our Lives Are Fulfilled by God's Unmerited Favor

42

TRUSTING GOD IN DIFFICULT TIMES

"Though he slay me, yet will I trust in him: but I will maintain my own ways before him." Job 13:15

1. Job Trusted God in Spite of Personal Loss
2. Job Trusted God in Spite of Personal Afflictions
3. Job Trusted God Even when God Was Silent

43

A LIGHT SHINING IN DARKNESS

"And the light shineth in darkness; and the darkness comprehended it not." John 1:5

1. The Perils of Walking in Darkness.
2. Jesus Is the Light of the World
3. The Joy of Walking in the Light

44

WHOLEHEARTED SERVICE

Romans 15:1–3

1. Service Rendered out of Love for God
2. Service Rendered to Make the World a Better Place
3. Service Rendered to Draw Men to God

45

A BRIDGE OVER TROUBLED WATERS

"Deliver me out of the mire, and let me not sink." Psalm 69:14

1. God Is a Bridge over the Waters of Sin
2. God Is a Bridge over the Waters of Alienation
3. God Is a Bridge over the Waters of Persecution

THE BIRTHMARKS OF THE CHURCH

"To the general assembly and church of the firstborn..."
Hebrews 12:23

1. The Birthmark of Suffering
2. The Birthmark of Redemption
3. The Birthmark of Witnessing

GOD IS ABLE

"Wherefore he is able also to save them to the uttermost that come unto God by him, seeing he ever liveth to make intercession for them." Hebrews 7:25

1. God Is Able to Comfort Us
2. God Is Able to Strengthen Us
3. God Is Able to Save Us

A PAUSE FOR POWER

"And they were all filled with the Holy Ghost, and began to speak with other tongues, as the Spirit gave them utterance." Acts 2:4

1. The Church Receives Strength when It Pauses for Power
2. The Church Receives Wisdom when It Pauses for Power
3. The Church Receives Courage when It Pauses for Power

WHOSE CHILD IS THIS?

"Behold a virgin shall be with child, and shall bring forth a son, and they shall call his name Emmanuel, which being interpreted is, God with us." Matthew 1:23

1. The Son of a Personal God
2. The Son of a Living God
3. The Son of a Loving God

50

WHAT IS MAN?

Psalm 8

1. Man Is God's Highest Creation
2. Man Is God's Fallen Creation
3. Man Is God's Redeemed Creation

51

THE SECRET PLACE

Psalm 91:1–4

1. Where the Shadow of God Falls on Us
2. Where God Is Our Eternal Refuge
3. Where God Exempts Us from Evil
4. Where God Has Ministering Angels (v. 11)

52

DELIVERANCE WILL COME

"If a man die, shall he live again? All the days of my appointed time will I wait, till my change come." Job 14:14

1. God Never Forsakes the Righteous
2. God's Grace Is Sufficient in Troubled Times
3. God Is Still on His Throne

53

COME BEFORE WINTER

"Do thy diligence to come before winter. . ." II Timothy 4:21

1. Come to Christ Before the Winter of Sin Sets In

2. Come to Christ Before the Winter of Trouble Sets In
3. Come to Christ Before the Winter of Suffering Sets In

54

DO WE NEED A SAVIOR?

"All we like sheep have gone astray; we have turned every one to his own way; and the Lord hath laid on him the iniquity of us all." Isaiah 53:6

1. We Need a Savior Because We Are Sinners
2. We Need a Savior Because Man's Way Is Insufficient
3. We Need a Savior to Reconcile Us to God

55

NEW MEN ON THE JERICHO ROAD

Luke 10:29–37

1. Men with the Right Intention
2. Men Whose Hearts Have Been Changed
3. Men Who Are Not Afraid to Deny Themselves

56

LIFE WITH THE RISEN LORD

John 20:19–21

1. Life with the Risen Lord Calms Our Fears
2. Life with the Risen Lord Restores Our Joys
3. Life with the Risen Lord Anchors Us in Hope

57

WHEN CHRIST IS WITH US

Matthew 28:19–20

1. We Go Unafraid

2. We Go with a Message of Love
3. We Go with the Knowledge of Divine Presence

58

NO GREATER LOVE

"Greater love hath no man than this, that a man lay down his life for his friends." John 15:13

1. No One Has Denied Himself More Than Christ
2. No One Has Cared More Than Christ
3. No Greater Sacrifice Has Been Made Than Christ

59

ECHOES OF A DESPERATE CRY

"In my distress I cried unto the Lord, and he heard me." Psalm 120:1

1. The Echoing Voice of Distress (In My Distress)
2. The Echoing Voice of Loneliness (I Cried)
3. The Echoing Voice of Deliverance (He Heard Me)

60

HOW MUCH HAVE YOU GIVEN?

Luke 21:1-4

1. Some Give Nothing
2. Some Give One-tenth
3. Some Give All

61

A TIME TO COME DOWN

"And when Jesus came to the place, he looked up, and saw him, and said unto him, Zacchaeus, make haste, and come down; for today I must abide at thy house." Luke 19:5

1. When the Master Demands Our Attention
2. When We Recognize Our Indebtedness to Others
3. When Death Knocks at the Door

62

WHY CHRIST HAD TO DIE

"Therefore the Jews sought the more to kill him, because he not only had broken the sabbath, but said also that God was his Father, making himself equal with God." John 5:18

Christ had to die because:
1. He Treated All Men the Same
2. He Led People Away from Traditional Religion
3. He Captured the Attention of the Multitude
4. He Was the Perfect Embodiment of His Father

63

THE PARABLE OF THE SOWER

Matthew 13:3–8

1. Some Seeds Fell by the Wayside
2. Some Seeds Fell on Stony Places
3. Some Seeds Fell Among Thorns
4. Some Seeds Fell on Good Ground

64

WILL THE LORD REMEMBER ME?

"And he said unto Jesus, Lord, remember me when thou comest into thy kingdom." Luke 23:42

The question implies:
1. A Consciousness of One's Own Sins
2. An Awareness of the Impending Judgment
3. Absolute Dependence on the Grace of God

DIVINE PROTECTION IN A DANGEROUS AGE

Psalm 91

1. God Is Our Refuge (v. 2)
2. God Is Our Deliverer (v. 3)
3. God Is Our Shield (v. 4)

IS THERE ANYONE TO HELP US?

John 5:1–11

1. There Is One Who Understands Our Hearts
2. There Is One Who Will Share Our Sorrows
3. There Is One Who Will Give a Sinner Pardon

I SHALL NOT BE MOVED

"He only is my rock and my salvation: he is my defence; I shall not be moved." Psalm 62:6

1. The Recognition That Salvation Comes from God
2. The Awareness That God Is His Only Defense
3. The Assurance That God Is Plenteous in Mercy

GOD'S WAY IS THE BEST WAY

Jonah 1:1–10

1. God's Way Is the Way of Love
2. God's Way Is the Way of Peace
3. God's Way Is the Way of Righteousness.
4. God's Way Is the Way of Forgiveness

69

DO YOU HAVE A VISION?

"Where there is no vision, the people perish..." Proverbs 29:18

1. A Vision Reveals the Unknown
2. A Vision Inspires Us to Persevere
3. A Vision Disciplines Our Hopes

70

THE BITTER CUP

"Saying, Father, if thou be willing, remove this cup from me: Nevertheless not my will, but thine, be done." Luke 22:42

1. The Cup Contained the Sins of Mankind
2. The Cup Would Take the Life of Christ
3. The Cup Represented the Justice of God
4. The Cup Enabled Mankind to Taste the Mercy of God

71

"THE THRILL HAS GONE"

"Restore unto me the joy of thy salvation; and uphold me with thy free spirit." Psalm 51:12

When the thrill has gone, one must:
1. Search for the Real Cause
2. Petition God for a Clean Heart
3. Hope for the Abiding Presence of God
4. Spread the News That the Thrill Has Returned

72

"FROM HERE TO ETERNITY"

"And Jesus said unto him, Verily I say unto thee, Today shalt thou be with me in paradise." Luke 23:43

The thief went:
1. From Sin to the Cross
2. From the Cross to Christ
3. With Christ into Eternity

73

THE BLOWING WINDS OF CHALLENGE

Job 38:1–3

1. The Challenge of Cognitive Power (v. 2)
2. The Challenge of Human Potentiality (v. 3)
3. The Challenge of Creative Power (v. 3)

74

THE SWELLING OF THE JORDAN

Jeremiah 12:5

Every life has its swelling Jordans:
1. When Popularity Exceeds Character
2. When Rituals Exceed Righteousness
3. When Hate Exceeds Love

75

JUDE'S CONCLUDING DOXOLOGY

"Now unto him that is able to keep you from falling, and to present you faultless before the presence of his glory with exceeding joy." Jude 1:24

1. Jude Offers Hope for a Troubled Church
2. Jude Reveals an Abiding Faith
3. Jude Points to a God Who Is Able

76

POWER FOR HIGHER HEIGHTS

"I can do all things through Christ which strengtheneth me."
Philippians 4:13

1. Power to Spread the Word under Adverse Circumstances
2. Power to Make Life Count for Good
3. Power to Hold On until the End

77

LIMITED VISIONS OF AN UNLIMITED SAVIOR

"Is not this the carpenter, the son of Mary, the brother of James, and Joses, and of Juda, and Simon? and are not his sisters here with us?" Mark 6:3

1. Some See Jesus as the Carpenter's Son
2. Some See Jesus as Mary's Baby Boy
3. Some See Jesus as a Prophet
4. Some See Jesus as a Savior

78

DO YOURSELF A FAVOR

Matthew 6:33–34

1. Seek God First in Your Life
2. Be Prepared to Accept God's Blessings
3. Don't Worry about Tomorrow

79

A FAITH THAT WILL NOT SHRINK

Hebrews 11:1

1. A Faith That Holds under Pressure

2. A Faith That Seeks a Closer Relationship
3. A Faith That Sustains Our Highest Hope

80

HAVE YOU SEEN HIS STAR?

"For we have seen his star in the east and are come to worship him." Matthew 2:2

1. When We See His Star We Are Filled with Joy (v. 10)
2. When We See His Star We Worship Him (v. 11)
3. When We See His Star We Offer Him Our Gifts (v. 11)
4. When We See His Star We Return Another Way (v. 12)

81

DIVINE COMPASSION: HELP FOR THE HELPLESS

"He giveth power to the faint; and to them that have no might he increaseth strength." Isaiah 40:29

1. Helplessness Is the Fallen Condition of Man
2. Compassion Is a Divine Attribute
3. Calvary Is the Height of Divine Compassion

82

GOD CARES FOR HIS OWN

"I have been young, and now am old; yet have I not seen the righteous forsaken, nor his seed begging bread." Psalm 37:25

1. By the Ordering of the Universe
2. By Allowing the Truth to Prevail
3. By Divine Intervention
4. By His Presence with Us

83

TRUST IN THE LORD

"Trust in the Lord, and do good; so shalt thou dwell in the land, and verily thou shalt be fed." Psalm 37:3

1. When We Trust God We Seek to Do Good
2. When We Trust God We Commit Our Lives to Him
3. When We Trust God We Delight in Him
4. When We Trust God We Exercise a Patient Spirit

84

DON'T FORGET GOD

"Remember now thy Creator in the days of thy youth. . . ." Ecclesiastes 12:1

1. Remember God While You Are Young
2. Remember God While the Days of Evil Are Far-off
3. Remember God While Life Is Yet Favorable

85

HOLD TO YOUR FAITH

"Fight the good fight of faith, lay hold on eternal life, whereunto thou art called, and hast professed a good profession before many witnesses." I Timothy 6:12

1. To Remain True to Your Calling from God
2. Someone Is Looking to You to Find the Way
3. You've Come Too Far to Turn Around
4. There Is a Promised Crown in Lay-away

86

SOMETHING TO BELIEVE IN

Isaiah 33:16-17

1. A Sure Defense from Evil (God)

2. An Adequate Supply of Daily Bread (God's Storehouse)
3. A King Shall Reign over Us (Jesus)

87

HAVE YOU FOUND CHRIST?

"Let us now go even unto Bethlehem, and see this thing which is come to pass, which the Lord hath made known unto us." Luke 2:15

If we are to find Christ:
1. We Must Listen to God's Messenger
2. We Must Seek Jesus with Haste
3. We Must Exhibit a Humble Spirit

88

WHEN GOD FOUND ME

Psalm 73:2–3

1. I Was Lost in Sin (My Feet Were Almost Gone)
2. I Could Not Help Myself (My Steps Had Well-nigh Slipped)
3. I Possessed a Misdirected Attitude (I Was Envious of the Foolish)

89

THE CHARGE TO THE PREACHER

II Timothy 4:1–5

1. Preach the Word
2. Watch All Things
3. Endure Afflictions
4. Make Full Proof of Your Ministry

90

A HARVEST OF SHAME

Luke 12:16–17

There is a harvest of shame:
1. When We Fail to Give God the Praise
2. When We Fail to Share Our Blessings
3. When We Confuse Self with Soul
4. When We Are Unable to Accept God's Goodness

91

SEARCH FOR TOMORROW

"Let us not be weary in well doing: for in due season we shall reap, if we faint not." Galatians 6:9

1. A Challenge (Be not weary in well doing)
2. A Promise (For in due season we shall reap)
3. A Warning (If we faint not)

92

BE OF GOOD CHEER

"But straightway Jesus spake unto them, saying, Be of good cheer; it is I; be not afraid." Matthew 14:27

We can be of good cheer because:
1. Christ Comes when Dangers Assail
2. Christ Speaks to Contrary Winds
3. Christ Acts to Still the Stormy Sea

93

THE POWER OF PRAYER

"And shall not God avenge his own elect, which cry day and night unto him, though he bear long with them?" Luke 18:7

1. Prayer Humbles the Person Who Prays

2. Prayer Keeps Our Needs Before God
3. Prayer Seeks a Divine Response
4. Prayer Strengthens the Person Who Prays

94

A PROPHET WITHOUT HONOR

"And they were offended in him. But Jesus said unto them, A prophet is not without honour, save in his own country, and in his own house." Matthew 13:57

Christ was without praise because:
1. He Preached the Truth
2. He Lived the Truth
3. He Was the Truth

95

THE EVERLASTING ARMS OF GOD

"The eternal God is thy refuge, and underneath are the everlasting arms." Deuteronomy 33:27

1. The Arms of God Made Us (Symbolic of God's Creativity)
2. The Arms of God Sustain Us (Symbolic of Divine Providence)
3. The Arms of God Saved Us (Symbolic of God's Love)

96

THE GUIDING LIGHT

"Then spake Jesus unto them, saying, I am the light of the world: he that followeth me shall not walk in darkness, but shall have the light of life." John 8:12

1. God's Light Keeps Us from the Path of Mental Darkness

2. God's Light Keeps Us from the Back Alley of Moral Darkness
3. God's Light Keeps Us from the Low Road of Spiritual Darkness

97

THE VALLEY OF DRY BONES

Ezekiel 37:1–11

1. Dry Bones Are Symbolic of Man's Waywardness
2. Dry Bones Are Symbolic of Dreams Deferred
3. Dry Bones Are Symbolic of Our Alienation from God
4. Dry Bones Are Symbolic of Our Helpless Condition
5. Dry Bones Are Symbolic of Man Without God's Word

98

THE VOICE OF PRAYER

"Then said Jesus, Father, forgive them; for they know not what they do." Luke 23:34

1. A Prayer to God as "Father"
2. A Prayer for His Enemies
3. A Prayer That Shows Faith in Life's Darkest Hour

99

GOD IS DOING GREAT THINGS

"The Lord hath done great things for us; whereof we are glad." Psalm 126:3

1. God Keeps Watch over Us Each Day
2. God Fills Us with an Abiding Joy
3. God Turns the Tides of Trouble Away from Us

100

COME AND DINE WITH CHRIST

"Jesus saith unto them, Come and dine. And none of the disciples durst ask him, Who art thou? knowing that it was the Lord." John 21:12

1. We Can Dine with Christ in an Atmosphere of Love
2. We Can Dine with Christ in an Atmosphere of Hope
3. We Can Dine with Christ in an Atmosphere of Grace
4. We Can Dine with Christ in an Atmosphere of Peace

101

WHERE IS YOUR FAITH?

"And he said unto them, Where is your faith? And they being afraid wondered, saying one to another, What manner of man is this! for he commandeth even the winds and water, and they obey him." Luke 8:25

1. Our Faith Should Be on the Growing Edge
2. Our Faith Should be Anchored to Christ
3. Our Faith Should Be a Light to Others
4. Our Faith Should Be the Basis of Our Hope

102

FAINTING SOULS AND RAGING SEAS

"When my soul fainted within me I remembered the Lord: and my prayer came in unto thee, into thine holy temple." Jonah 2:7

1. Our Souls Faint when We Disobey God
2. Raging Seas Are Often the Birthplace for Prayer
3. Fainting Souls and Raging Seas Are Subject to God

103

PUSHED TO THE OUTER LIMITS

"And the night following the Lord stood by him, and said, Be of good cheer, Paul: for as thou hast testified of me in Jerusalem, so must thou bear witness also at Rome." Acts 23:11

Paul was pushed to the outer limits because:
1. To Whom Much Is Given, Much Is Required
2. Christ Must Be Crowned Lord of All
3. Christian Witnessing Must Transcend Every Barrier

104

"THE CROSS OF CHRISTIAN DISCIPLESHIP"

"Then said Jesus unto his disciples, If any man will come after me, let him deny himself, and take up his cross, and follow me." Matthew 16:24

1. The Cross of Christian Discipleship Requires Self-denial
2. The Cross of Christian Discipleship Must Be Freely Taken Up
3. The Cross of Christian Discipleship Prepares Us for the Worst
4. The Cross of Christian Discipleship Equips Us for the Best

105

FOR THIS CAUSE

"Pilate therefore said unto him, Art thou a king then? Jesus answered, Thou sayest that I am a king. To this end was I born, and for this cause came I into the world, that I should bear witness unto the truth. Every one that is of the truth heareth my voice." John 18:37

1. Christ Came to Fulfill the Law
2. Christ Came to Bear Witness to the Truth
3. Christ Came to Offer Eternal Life to All
4. Christ Came to Offer Abundant Living

106
A NEW COMMANDMENT

"A new commandment I give unto you, That ye love one another; as I have loved you, that ye also love one another. By this shall all men know that ye are my disciples, if ye have love one to another." John 13:34–35

1. The New Commandment Was Given by a Loving Christ
2. The New Commandment Called for Christlike Love
3. The New Commandment Is Symbolic of Our Commitment to Christ

107
CASE DISMISSED

"When Jesus had lifted up himself, and saw none but the woman, he said unto her, Woman, where are thine accusers? hath no man condemned thee?" John 8:10

The case against the adulterous woman was dismissed because:
1. Christ Became the Chief Counsel for Her Defense
2. Each Witness Was Disqualified
3. Christ Instituted a Workable Rehabilitation Program

108
WISDOM'S OPEN INVITATION

"Whoso is simple, let him turn in hither: as for him that wanteth understanding, she saith to him, Come, eat of my

bread, and drink of the wine which I have mingled." Proverbs 9:4-5

Wisdom is a divine attribute:
1. Wisdom Openly Invites the Simple
2. Wisdom Serves the Bread of Truth
3. Wisdom Mixes the Wine of Righteousness

109

HOW LONG WILL YOUR JOURNEY BE?

"And the king said unto me, (the queen also sitting by him,) For how long shall the journey be? and when wilt thou return? So it pleased the king to send me; and I set him a time." Nehemiah 2:6

1. From the Wilderness of Sin to the Plains of Righteousness
2. From the Strange Land of Captivity to the Homeland of Freedom
3. From Earthly Tents to the City Not Made with Hands

110

WHEN GOD IS WITH US

"There shall not any man be able to stand before thee all the days of thy life: as I was with Moses, so I will be with thee: I will not fail thee, nor forsake thee." Joshua 1:5

1. We Can Maintain Courage Through Difficult Times
2. Our Strength Is Renewed Through the Crisis
3. We Look Forward to the Fulfillment of Divine Promises

111

THE STORMS OF ADVERSE CIRCUMSTANCES

Matthew 7:24-27

Life has many storms:
1. The Beating Rains of Trouble

2. The Flowing Waters of Sin
3. The Chilling Winds of Fear

112

ONE WAY OUT

"Now the days of David drew nigh that he should die; and he charged Solomon his son, saying, I go the way of all the earth: by thou strong therefore, and shew thyself a man." I Kings 2:1–2

1. Death Is the Only Way Out for the Rich Man in His Mansion
2. Death Is the Only Way Out for the King in His Royal Palace
3. Death Is the Only Way Out for the Poor Man in His Shanty
4. Death Is the Only Way Out for Those Who Enjoy the Pleasures
5. Death Is the Only Way Out for the Righteous Who Walk with God

113

THAT THEY MAY BE ONE

"And now I am no more in the world, but these are in the world, and I come to thee. Holy Father, keep those whom thou hast given me, that they may be one, as we are." John 17:11

Jesus prayed that His disciples would be one because:
1. Disciples of Christ Should Be One in Love
2. Disciples of Christ Should Be One in Prayer
3. Disciples of Christ Should Be One in Faith
4. Disciples of Christ Should Be One in Service

114

A CHOSEN VESSEL

"But the Lord said unto them, Go thy way: for he is a chosen vessel unto me, to bear my name before the Gentiles, and kings, and the children of Israel: For I will shew him how great things he must suffer for my name's sake." Acts 9:15–16

1. God's Chosen Vessels Are Called to Break New Ground
2. God's Chosen Vessels Are Appointed a Chosen Task
3. God's Chosen Vessels Must Suffer for His Sake

115

THE HAND OF THE LORD

"And the hand of the Lord was with them: and a great number believed, and turned unto the Lord." Acts 11:21

The hand of the Lord is upon each church that:
1. Continues to Witness Under Pressure
2. Lives According to Divine Guidance
3. Preaches Christ as God's Remedy for Sin
4. Gives to God His Due Praise

116

A NEW WAY

"Jesus saith unto him, I am the way, the truth, and the life: no man cometh unto the Father, but by me." John 14:6

Jesus is our new way:
1. A New Way to Triumph over Trouble
2. A New Way to Triumph over Fear
3. A New Way to Triumph over Sin
4. A New Way to Triumph over Death

117

WHERE IS YOUR TREASURE?

"For where your treasure is, there will your heart be also."
Luke 12:34

1. Some Men Trust the Fading Treasures of Silver and Gold
2. Some Men Covet the Treasure of Academic Excellence
3. Some Men Attempt to Accumulate Treasures in Heaven Through Good Deeds

118

INVESTMENTS IN THE DIVINE ECONOMY

"Then answered Peter and said unto him, Behold, we have forsaken all, and followed thee; what shall we have therefore?" Matthew 19:27

1. Some Investments Offer No Return
2. Other Investments Allow Us to Break Even
3. A Few Investments Offer a Rich Return
4. Our Investments with God Bring Eternal Life

119

THE MATCHLESS LOVE OF GOD

"Behold, what manner of love the Father hath bestowed upon us, that we should be called the sons of God: therefore the world knoweth us not, because it knew him not." I John 3:1

1. God's Love Is Capable of Looking Beyond Our Faults
2. God's Love Was Expressed while We Were Yet Sinners
3. God's Love Bestows a Rich Heritage on Us

120

AN INQUISITIVE MIND

"Teach me, O Lord, the way of thy statutes; and I shall keep it unto the end." Psalm 119:33

1. An Inquisitive Mind Seeks Divine Guidance
2. An Inquisitive Mind Seeks a Clear Understanding
3. An Inquisitive Mind Combines the Assets of Heart and Head

121

CAN ANY GOOD THING COME OUT OF NAZARETH?

"And Nathanael said unto him, Can there any good thing come out of Nazareth? Phillip said unto him, Come and see."
John 1:46

1. A Wonderful Counselor Came Out of Nazareth
2. A Friend to All Humanity Came Out of Nazareth
3. The King of Kings Came Out of Nazareth
4. The Savior of the World Came Out of Nazareth

122

THINK ON THESE THINGS

"Finally, brethren, whatsoever things are true, whatsoever things are honest, whatsoever things are just, whatsoever things are pure, whatsoever things are lovely, whatsoever things are of good report; if there be any virtue, and if there be any praise, think on these things." Philippians 4:8

1. Whatsoever Things Are Honest
2. Whatsoever Things Are Just
3. Whatsoever Things Are Pure
4. Whatsoever Things Are Lovely
5. Whatsoever Things Are of Good Report

123

A VIEW FROM THE INSIDE

"And ye are witnesses of these things." Luke 24:48

1. A View from the Inside Gives Us a Picture of the Person of Christ

2. A View from the Inside Gives Us a Picture of the Works of Christ
3. A View from the Inside Gives Us a Picture of the Promises of Christ

124

DOORKEEPERS TO HOLY PLACES

"I had rather be a doorkeeper in the house of my God, than to dwell in the tents of wickedness." Psalm 84:10

There is joy in being a doorkeeper because:
1. Doorkeepers Are Able to Hear the Word of God
2. Doorkeepers Are Able to Experience the Presence of God
3. Doorkeepers Are Able to Feel the Power of God
4. Doorkeepers Are Saved by the Grace of God

125

WHICH SIDE ARE YOU ON?

"He that is not with me is against me: and he that gathereth not with me scattereth." Luke 11:23

Biblical history shows us that:
1. There Are Two Sides to Life
2. We Are Free to Choose Either Side
3. Christ's Side Will Be Victorious

126

THE PATHS OF GOD

"All the paths of the Lord are mercy and truth unto such as keep his covenant and his testimonies." Psalm 25:10

1. The Path of God Is "Plain."
2. The Path of God is "Love."
3. The Path of God is "Truth."

127

THE GREAT COMMANDMENT

"Master, which is the great commandment in the law? Jesus said unto him, Thou shalt love the Lord thy God with all thy heart, and with all thy soul, and with all thy mind." Matthew 22:36–37

The great commandment calls for a total response:
1. We Are to Love God with All Our Heart
2. We Are to Love God with All Our Soul
3. We Are to Love God with All Our Mind

128

PERSEVERANCE IN PRAYER

"And I say unto you, Ask, and it shall be given you; seek, and ye shall find; knock, and it shall be opened unto you." Luke 11:9

1. God Wants Us to Ask when We Are in Need
2. God Wants Us to Seek That Which Is Productive to Life
3. God Wants Us to Knock on the Doors of Opportunity

129

WE GLORY IN TRIBULATIONS

"And not only so, but we glory in tribulations also: knowing that tribulation worketh patience; and patience, experience, and experience, hope. . ." Romans 5:3–4

1. Tribulations Lead to Patience
2. Patience Helps Us to Gain Experience
3. Experience Reassures Our Hope

130

SOMETHING TO HOLD ONTO

"Let love be without dissimulation. Abhor that which is evil; cleave to that which is good." Romans 12:9

1. Hold On to Love Because It Is Fulfilling
2. Hold On to Faith Because It Inspires
3. Hold On to Truth Because It Sets You Free
4. Hold On to Jesus Because He Can Save You

131

THIS I KNOW

"Behold, I shew you a mystery; We shall not all sleep, but we shall all be changed." I Corinthians 15:51

1. We Shall Not All Sleep
2. We Shall All Be Changed
3. The Dead Shall Be Raised Incorruptible
4. The Victory Over Death Is Given Through Jesus

132

LOOK ON US

"And Peter, fastening his eyes upon him with John, said, Look on us." Acts 3:4

Look on us and see that:
1. Our Faith Exceeds Our Finance
2. Our Trust Exceeds Our Trials
3. Our Prudence Exceeds Our Poverty

133

COME OUT OF THE WILDERNESS

"And they took their journey from Elim, and all the congregation of the children of Israel came into the wilderness of Sin,

which is between Elim and Sinai, on the fifteenth day of the second month after their departing out of the land of Egypt. And the whole congregation of the children of Israel murmured against Moses and Aaron in the wilderness." Exodus 16:1-2

We need to come out of the wilderness because:
1. There Is Always a Place Called Sin in the Wilderness
2. Religious Leadership Is Often Defied in the Wilderness
3. The Wilderness Can Cause Us to Lose Sight of Our Goal
4. The Promised Land Is Beyond the Wilderness

134

A RENEWED MIND

"And be not conformed to this world: but be ye transformed by the renewing of your mind, that ye may prove what is that good, and acceptable, and perfect, will of God." Romans 12:2

1. A Renewed Mind Seeks That Which Is Good
2. A Renewed Mind Seeks That Which Is Acceptable
3. A Renewed Mind Seeks to Discover the Will of God

135

IN THE TIME OF TROUBLE

"For in the time of trouble he shall hide me in his pavilion: in the secret of his tabernacle shall he hide me; he shall set me up upon a rock." Psalm 27:5

1. God Hides Us in His Pavilion
2. The Tabernacle of God Becomes a Spiritual Stronghold
3. God Moves to Higher Heights

136

THE AFFLICTIONS OF THE RIGHTEOUS

"Many are the afflictions of the righteous: but the Lord delivereth him out of them all." Psalm 34:19

1. The Righteous Are Not Exempt from Trouble
2. Christian Character Is Strengthened Through Afflictions
3. God Is Able to Help Us Through All Afflictions

137

THE STRENGTH OF SOLITUDE

"And when he had sent the multitudes away, he went up into a mountain apart to pray: and when the evening was come, he was there alone." Matthew 14:23

1. Solitude Allows Us to Reflect
2. Solitude Helps Us to Heal Our Broken Hearts
3. Solitude Strengthens Us for the Tasks Ahead

138

THE CITY OF OUR GOD

"Great is the Lord, and greatly to be praised in the city of our God, in the mountain of his holiness." Psalm 48:1

1. The City of God Is Wherever God Reigns Supreme in the Human Heart
2. The City of God Is Wherever We Experience the Lovingkindness of God
3. The City of God Is a Perpetual Fortress Against Evil Forces

139

PERFECT PEACE

"Thou shalt keep him in perfect peace, whose mind is stayed on thee: because he trusteth in thee." Isaiah 26:3

1. Only God Can Give Perfect Peace
2. Peace Is the Offspring of Trust
3. Perfect Peace Takes Place in Spite of External Conflicts

140

A COMFORTING VOICE IN AN ALIEN LAND

"Comfort ye, comfort ye my people, saith your God. Speak ye comfortably to Jerusalem, and cry unto her, that her warfare is accomplished, that her iniquity is pardoned..." Isaiah 40:1-2

1. God's Voice Assures Us That We Are Never Alone
2. God's Voice Tells Us That We Are Merely Pilgrims
3. Alien Lands Make Us More Attentive to the Voice of God

141

HAVE YOU BEEN THROUGH THE FLOODS?

"When thou passest through the waters, I will be with thee: And through the rivers, they shall not overflow thee: when thou walkest through the fire, thou shalt not be burned; neither shall the flame kindle upon thee." Isaiah 43:2

1. The Floods of Life Help Us to Realize Our Limitations
2. The Floods of Life Force Us to Reach Out to God
3. The Floods of Life Reveal the Saving Grace of God

142

THE LOW ROAD TO HIGH PLACES

"Be afflicted, and mourn, and weep: let your laughter be turned to mourning, and your joy to heaviness. Humble yourselves in the sight of the Lord, and he shall lift you up." James 4:9-10

1. The Low Road of Suffering Often Leads to Increased Faith
2. The Low Road of Mourning Leads to Divine Comfort
3. The Low Road of Humility Leads to Divine Exaltation

143

A TOUCH OF CLASS

"And, behold, a woman in the city, which was a sinner, when she knew that Jesus sat at meat in the Pharisee's house, brought an alabaster box of ointment, and stood at his feet behind him weeping, and began to wash his feet with tears, and did wipe them with the hairs of her head, and kissed his feet, and anointed them with the ointment." Luke 7:37–38

A touch of class is exemplified:
1. Whenever We Recognize Our Own Shortcomings
2. Whenever Repentant Sinners Weep at Jesus' Feet
3. Whenever Divine Pardon Takes Place

144

THE WAY OF THE RIGHTEOUS

"For the Lord knoweth the way of the righteous: but the way of the ungodly shall perish." Psalm 1:6

1. The Righteous Delight in the Law of the Lord
2. The Way of the Righteous Is a Happy Path
3. The Way of the Righteous Is Known by God

145

DON'T FORGET THE FRAGMENTS

"And they took up twelve baskets full of the fragments, and of the fishes." Mark 6:43

Gathered fragments remind us that:
1. Another Day of Need Will Surely Come
2. The Blessings of God Should Not Be Wasted
3. Grateful Hearts Make Full Use of God's Blessings

146

A SONG OF VICTORY

"Then sang Moses and the children of Israel this song unto the Lord, and spake saying, I will sing unto the Lord, for he has triumphed gloriously: the horse and his rider hath he thrown into the sea." Exodus 15:1

1. A Song of Victory Acknowledges the Mighty Acts of God
2. A Song of Victory Celebrates God's Power over Evil
3. A Song of Victory Reminds Us That God Shall Reign Forever

147

BITTER WATERS MADE SWEET

"And he cried unto the Lord; and the Lord shewed him a tree, which when he had cast into the waters, the waters were made sweet" Exodus 15:25

1. God Can Make the Bitter Waters of Affliction Sweet
2. God Can Make the Bitter Waters of Suffering Sweet
3. God Can Make the Bitter Waters of Trouble Sweet

148

THE DIVINE LAW OF SUPPLY AND DEMAND

"But my God shall supply all your need according to his riches in glory by Christ Jesus." Philippians 4:19

1. The Demand—The Needs of the Righteous
2. The Storehouse—His Riches in Glory
3. The Supply—God Supplies All Your Needs
4. The Medium—Christ, Our Medium for Blessings

149

SONGS OF DELIVERANCE

"Thou art my hiding place; thou shalt preserve me from trouble; thou shalt compass me about with songs of deliverance." Psalm 32:7

1. Songs of Deliverance Express Our Deepest Sorrows
2. Songs of Deliverance Express Our Highest Hopes
3. Songs of Deliverance Express Our Dynamic Faith

150

COUNTED AMONG THE LOSERS

"But what things were gain to me, those I counted loss for Christ." Philippians 3:7

By worldly standards, Paul was among the losers because:
1. He Disregarded His Personal Heritage
2. He Forsook the Laws of the Pharisees
3. He Abandoned the Zeal of Persecution
4. He Followed a Crucified Lord

151

THE LAST PROCESSION
(A memorial to Rev. J. B. Friday)

"Thou hast a few names even in Sardis which have not defiled their garments; and they shall walk with me in white: for they are worthy." Revelation 3:4

The last procession is for:
1. Those Who Have Not Defiled Their Garments
2. Those Who Have Kept Watch by Day and Night
3. Those Who Are Worthy of Salvation
4. Those Whom Christ Shall Present Before God

152

A MIRACLE AT A MARRIAGE

"And the third day there was a marriage in Cana of Galilee; and the mother of Jesus was there: And both Jesus was called, and his disciples, to the marriage." John 2:1-2

1. A Bride and Groom Who Wanted Jesus Present
2. A Bride and Groom Who Needed the Presence of Jesus
3. A Bride and Groom Who Were Blessed by the Presence of Jesus

153

A GOOD SOLDIER OF JESUS CHRIST

"Thou therefore endure hardness, as a good soldier of Jesus Christ." II Timothy 2:3

1. A Good Soldier Keeps That Which Is Entrusted to Him
2. A Good Soldier Keeps His Oath under Pressure
3. A Good Soldier Remains at His Post until Relieved of Duty
4. A Good Soldier Receives Commendation from the Chief of Staff

154

A MORE EXCELLENT NAME

"Being made so much better than the angels, as he hath by inheritance obtained a more excellent name than they." Hebrews 1:4

1. Jesus—The Only Begotten of God
2. Jesus—The Prince of Peace
3. Jesus—The Wonderful Counselor
4. Jesus—The Savior of the World

155

EYE WITNESSES TO HOLY EVENTS

"Behold my hands and my feet, that it is I myself: handle me and see; for a spirit hath not flesh and bones, as ye see me have." Luke 24:39

1. Eye Witnesses to Holy Events Are a Privileged Few
2. Eye Witnesses to Holy Events Have a Missionary Obligation
3. Eye Witnesses to Holy Events Have a Personal Testimony

156

WHAT DO YOU WANT FROM JESUS?

"Then Jesus turned, and saw them following, and saith unto them, what seek ye? They said unto him, Rabbi (which is to say, being interpreted, Master) where dwellest thou?" John 1:38

1. Some People Follow Jesus for Personal Gain
2. Some People Follow Jesus for Social Recognition
3. Some People Follow Jesus for Personal Salvation

157

THE WHOLE TRUTH

"For God so loved the world, that he gave his only begotten Son, that whosoever believeth in him should not perish, but have everlasting life." John 3:16

1. A Divine Face—"God so loved the world"
2. Divine Love Expressed—"He gave his only begotten Son"
3. The Divine Purpose—"Whosoever believeth in him should not perish"
4. The Divine Goal—"But have everlasting life"

158

THE DIVIDENDS OF CHRISTIAN BELIEFS

"Verily, verily, I say unto you, he that heareth my word, and believeth on him that sent me, hath everlasting life, and shall not come into condemnation; but is passed from death unto life." John 5:24

1. Hearing and Believing Are Our Initial Investments
2. Our Investments Prevent Spiritual Condemnation
3. Eternal Life Is Our Compounded Interest
4. Dwelling with God Will Be Our Highest Yield

159

THE JOY OF FOLLOWING JESUS

"And he saith unto them, follow me, and I will make you fishers of men." Matthew 4:19

1. He Who Follows Jesus Discovers an Inward Peace
2. He Who Follows Jesus Discovers the Will of God
3. He Who Follows Jesus Discovers the Reward of God

160

DON'T LET JESUS DOWN

"From that time many of his disciples went back, and walked no more with him. Then said Jesus unto the twelve, Will ye also go away?" John 6:66-67

We should not let Jesus down because:
1. He Is Counting on Us
2. He Is Our Only Hope
3. He Did Not Let Us Down

161

GOOD INTENTIONS ON LIFE'S WRONG ROADS

"And not many days after the younger son gathered all to-gether, and took his journey into a far country, and there wasted his substance with riotous living." Luke 15:13

Good intentions on the wrong roads of life made the wayward son:
1. A Failure from the Outset
2. A Product of Bad Company
3. An Alien in a Far Country

162

GOD ALWAYS HAS A WAY OUT

"And the Lord said unto Moses, wherefore criest thou unto me? speak unto the children of Israel, that they go forward." Exodus 14:15

God always has a way out for His people
1. Faith Is God's Way Out of Doubt
2. Hope Is God's Way Out of Despair
3. Jesus Is God's Way Out of Sin

163

NEW MEN FOR GOD'S BOLD MISSION

Judges 7

The characteristics of the new men for God's bold mission are found in Gideon's army:
1. New Men for God's Bold Mission Are Courageous (v. 3)
2. New Men for God's Bold Mission Are Disciplined (v. 6)
3. New Men for God's Bold Mission Are Loyal (v. 21)

164

DON'T UNDERESTIMATE GOD

"Thus saith the Lord, Because the Syrians have said, the Lord is God of the hills, but he is not God of the valleys, therefore will I deliver all this great multitude into thine hand, and ye shall know that I am the Lord." I Kings 20:28

We underestimate God when:
1. We Misunderstand the Wisdom of an All-wise God
2. We Overlook the One Who Possesses All Power

165

THE KING WHO FORGOT THE GOLDEN RULE

"And thou shalt speak unto him, saying, Thus saith the Lord, Hast thou killed, and also taken possession? And thou shalt speak unto him, saying, Thus saith the Lord, In the place where dogs licked the blood of Naboth shall dogs lick thy blood, even thine." I Kings 21:19

1. The Cause—Greed for His Neighbor's Vineyard (v. 2)
2. The Plan—Take Naboth Away from His Vineyard (v. 13)
3. Divine Intervention—Wrong Never Pays (v. 19)
4. The Eternal Court of Justice—A Flying Arrow (v. 34)

166

THE WHOLE ARMOR OF GOD

Ephesians 6:11–17

The Christian is at war against sin and evil. Each Christian is a soldier in God's army. Any man who goes to a war knows the value of the proper armor. God provides the armor for those who serve in his army. The Christian is required to take up and utilize the whole armor of God. The armor of God consists of:
1. The Garment of Truth
2. The Breastplate of Righteousness

3. The Shoes of the Gospel of Peace
4. The Shield of Faith
5. The Helmet of Salvation
6. The Sword of the Spirit

167

HINDRANCES TO ABUNDANT LIVING

"But Naaman was wroth, and went away, and said, Behold, I thought, He will surely come out to me, and stand, and call on the name of the Lord his God, and strike his hand over the place, and recover the leper." II Kings 5:11

Most of the hindrances to abundant living are within us. Naaman discovered that such was the case in his own life. God had provided the means by which Naaman could be cured of his leprosy, but Naaman's attitude proved to be his greatest hindrance to abundant living. Certain hindrances still prevent us from enjoying life as fully as possible:
1. Excessive Pride
2. A Jealous Spirit
3. A Deceitful Heart
4. Love of Strife

168

WHAT A DIFFERENCE A DAY MAKES

"Boast not thyself of tomorrow: for thou knowest not what a day may bring forth." Proverbs 27:1

A popular tune has as its title, "What a Difference a Day Makes." The lyrics indicate that because of his acquaintance with the "dream lady" of his life, the singer's life has taken on a new dimension. While we as Christians are cautioned against boasting about tomorrow, there are some days of great significance to us.

1. The "Yesterday" of Regeneration
2. The "Today" of Suffering
3. The "Tomorrow" of Heavenly Glory

169

GOD'S GIFTS FOR PASTORAL LEADERSHIP

"For God hath not given us the spirit of fear: but of power, and of love, and of a sound mind." II Timothy 1:7

1. Power—The Ability to Preach with Conviction
2. Love—The Capacity of Ultimate Concern
3. A Sound Mind—The Mechanism for Right Reasoning

170

PATTERNS OF GOOD WORKS

"In all things shewing thyself a pattern of good works: in doctrine shewing uncorruptness, gravity, sincerity, sound speech, that cannot be condemned; that he, that is of the contrary part may be ashamed, having no evil thing to say of you." Titus 2:7-8

The Christian is called on to make his life a pattern for others to see and follow. There is no greater challenge for the Christian than to live so that his life can be viewed as a pattern of good works. There are those who are looking to us as patterns for:

1. Sound Doctrine
2. Dignified Conduct
3. Sound Speech
4. Sacrificial Living

171

IF

1. The "If" of Love

"If God so loved us, we ought also to love one another."
(I John 4:11)

2. The "If" of Faith

"If ye have faith as a grain of mustard seed, ye shall say unto this mountain, Remove hence to yonder place." Matthew 17:20

3. The "If" of Perfection

"If thou wilt be perfect, go and sell that thou hast, and give to the poor, and thou shalt have treasure in heaven: and come and follow me." Matthew 19:21

4. The "If" of Divine Providence

"If then God so clothe the grass, which is today in the field, and tomorrow is cast into the oven; how much more will he clothe you?" Luke 12:28

172

THE GREATEST OF THESE IS LOVE

I Corinthians 13

1. Love Is Greater Than the Silver Tongue of the Orator
2. Love Is Greater Than Prophetic Ability
3. Love Is Greater Than Mature Faith
4. Love Is Greater Than the Giving of Gifts
5. Love Is Greater Than Posthumous Honors Won Through Self-sacrificing

173

GOD STILL OPENS CLOSED DOORS

"And at midnight Paul and Silas prayed, and sang praises unto God: and the prisoners heard them. And suddenly there

was a great earthquake, so that the foundations of the prison were shaken: and immediately all the doors were opened, and every one's bands were loosed." Acts 16:25-26

1. God Opens the Doors to Personal Freedom
2. God Opens the Doors to Abundant Living
3. God Opens the Doors to Personal Salvation
4. God Opens the Doors to Christian Witnessing

174

THE GOODNESS OF GOD

"The Lord is good to all: and his tender mercies are over all his works." Psalm 145:9

1. The Person of God: God Is Good
2. The Inclusiveness of God's Goodness: To All
3. The Relationship of Goodness to God: Inseparable

175

GOD'S CARE OF THE RIGHTEOUS

"Blessed is he that considereth the poor: the Lord will deliver him in time of trouble:" Psalm 4:1

1. God Delivers the Righteous in Times of Trouble
2. God Preserves the Righteous in Times of Adversity
3. God Strengthens the Righteous in Times of Weakness
4. God Is Merciful Toward the Righteous in Times of Need